AUI

VALLEYS AND CANYONS

A TRUE BOOK

by

Larry Dane Brimner

Children's Press®

A Division of Grolier Publishing

New York London Hong Kong Sydney
Danbury, Connecticut

A valley below the
Himalayas in Tibet

Subject Consultant
Peter Goodwin
*Science Teacher, Kent School,
Kent, Connecticut*

Reading Consultant
Linda Cornwell
*Coordinator of School Quality
and Professional Improvement
Indiana State Teachers
Association*

Author's Dedication:
*For all my Happy Valley
Primary School friends*

Visit Children's Press® on the
Internet at:
http://publishing.grolier.com

*The photograph on the cover
shows the Grand Canyon. The
photograph on the title page
shows a river valley in Nepal.*

Library of Congress Cataloging-in-Publication Data

Brimner, Larry Dane
    Valleys and Canyons: a true book / by Larry Dane Brimner.
       p. cm. — (A true book)
    Includes bibliographical references and index.
    Summary: Describes different kinds of valleys and canyons and how
they are formed.
    ISBN 0-516-21569-8 (lib.bdg.)   0-516-27193-8 (pbk.)
    1. Valleys—Juvenile literature. 2. Canyons—Juvenile literature.
[1. Valleys. 2. Canyons.] I. Title. II. Series.
    GB561 .B75 2000
    551.44'2—dc21
                                        99-058399
                                             CIP
                                             AC

GROLIER
PUBLISHING

Contents

A valley at Olympic National Park in Washington

Peaks and Valleys

From a soaring mountain peak, a hiker looks down upon a green valley. Wherever there are mountain peaks, there are valleys below them. Valleys are the low places between highlands, hills, or mountains.

The Earth has many kinds of valleys. They range from

Bryce Canyon in Utah

canyons and gorges to rift valleys and glacial valleys, as well as the valleys we know best—river valleys. Valleys are found on every continent, and even under the sea. Some valleys are wide and flat, with gently sloping sides. Others are deep and steep-sided gouges in the Earth. Why are valleys different from one another? Let's take a closer look and find out.

A glacial valley in Iceland

How Valleys Become Valleys

Scientists believe the rocky outer shell of the Earth "floats" on a layer of super-hot liquid rock called magma. This outer shell—the lithosphere—is not a solid chunk of rock, however. It is broken into eight major pieces, or

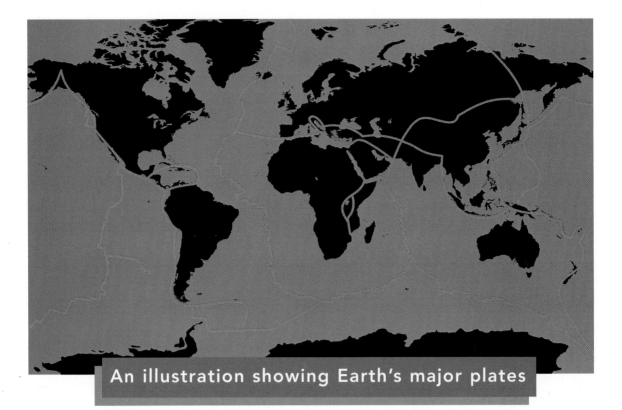

An illustration showing Earth's major plates

plates, and several smaller
ones.

These plates are always in
motion, but they move so
slowly that we do not usually
notice. Some of the world's

Valleys lie below folded mountains such as these in Alberta, Canada.

mountains were formed when these plates pushed against each other, causing great waves of rock to rise above the surrounding land. Such mountains are called folded mountains. The areas next to these mountains that were not pushed up became valleys.

As Earth's plates have moved, they have made long cracks, or faults, in the Earth's crust. Huge blocks of rock on either side of the faults may push up or slip

As the Earth's plates move, huge blocks of rock may push up or slip down.

down, forming fault-block mountains. Many of the mountains in western North America were formed this way. The basins, or hollows, next to the faults formed valleys.

A valley below the Grand Tetons, a fault-block mountain range in Wyoming

A valley below Mount Ararat, a volcanic mountain in Turkey

Mountains also formed when magma pushed under the Earth's crust to form large domes. The magma then exploded out of openings, or vents, in the lithosphere to form volcanoes. The lowlands surrounding these volcanic mountains became valleys.

Valleys are always connected to the hills and mountains that border them. But other forces also help to form and shape valleys.

River Valleys

The classic valley begins when rain falls. It flows down the hill-sides and into a channel. There, it forms a river and follows the shortest, easiest path to the sea.

The river cuts away at the bottom of the channel and makes it deeper. The fine sand, or sediment, at the bottom of

A river valley
in Colorado

the channel mixes with the water
and is carried away. Later, this
sediment drops out of the water
and settles where the river ends.

If the river were the only force wearing away, or eroding, the land, it would cut a deep gash with straight up-and-down sides. However, other elements—such as rain and frost—are wearing away the sides of the channel while the river is cutting it deeper. These other elements work to slope the sides and form a wide, V-shaped valley.

Eventually, the sides will be worn flat and the valley becomes a broad plain like the

The Mississippi River Valley in Mississippi

Mississippi River Valley. Then the river will no longer rush downhill. Instead, it will flow sluggishly to the sea.

Glacial Valleys

At many times during Earth's history, the climate has been much colder than it is now. During these cold spells, or ice ages, ice stretched down from the polar regions to cover large areas of the planet. The great weight of the ice made it flow like a slow-moving river.

A modern-day glacier in Alaska

These rivers of ice, or glaci-ers, were like giant bulldozers. As they pushed downhill, they plucked huge boulders from

In many parts of the world, huge valleys have been carved out by glaciers.

the ground and carved out deep valleys.

Glacial valleys aren't V-shaped like the valleys cut by rivers. Instead, they are shaped like the letter U. This is because glaciers eroded the sides as well as the bottoms of their rocky, ice-filled channels.

Glacial valleys are U-shaped, not V-shaped.

Some glacial valleys have been filled by fjords.

When the ice age ended and Earth warmed, the glaciers melted. The melting ice then raised the levels of the oceans. This caused glacial valleys along the coasts to fill with seawater, which created fjords, or inlets. Some fjords are more than 4,000 feet (1,219 meters) deep!

Glaciers are active today, but only in places where it is very cold. These glaciers are busy carving valleys of their own, just like the glaciers of long ago.

Rift Valleys

Rift valleys, which are also called grabens, are not made by erosion. They are made by faulting action—the movement of Earth's plates. Rift valleys occur between faults that are parallel to each other. When the plates move apart, the ground between the faults slips down to form valleys.

The Great Rift Valley in Africa

Africa's Great Rift Valley is the largest rift valley on any of the large landmasses we call continents. It is about 4,036 miles (6,458 kilometers) long and drops far below sea level.

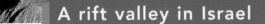
A rift valley in Israel

Scientists think the Great Rift Valley is continuing to form. Some of them believe that in millions of years it may split eastern Africa off from the rest of Africa to form a new continent.

Gorges

Water is one of nature's most powerful tools. Frozen water can chip away rock and bulldoze deep glacial valleys. As a liquid, water can shape river valleys and fill them with rich sediment that is ideal for growing crops. But water is also responsible for much erosion beneath the Earth's surface.

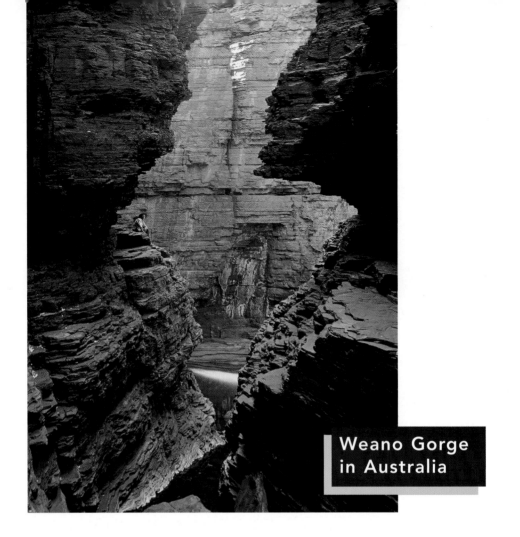

Weano Gorge
in Australia

As rain falls to Earth, it picks
up a gas called carbon dioxide. This is the gas that people
and animals breathe out. It is

also the gas given off by dead and decaying plants. So, as the rain seeps into the soil, it picks up even more carbon dioxide. The rain and carbon dioxide mix together to make carbonic acid.

Over millions of years, this acid is able to dissolve limestone, a soft rock made from the tightly-packed skeletons of tiny sea creatures. Eventually, however, the acid water drains away and air enters the hollow

A limestone cave

left behind. An underground cave has been made.

It may remain a cave for a very long time, but rainwater continues to trickle through its roof. Eventually, the roof may

The Flume, a gorge in New Hampshire

grow weak and crumble. Now the cave has become a gorge.

The term "gorge" may be used to describe any small, narrow canyon with steep sides, but it often refers to those

A natural stone bridge arching across a gorge

places formed from collapsed caves. Sometimes, a natural stone bridge may arch across the gorge. Once, the bridge may have formed part of a cave's roof. Now it links one side of the gorge with the other.

Canyons

Canyons are valleys formed by river erosion, but they are different from classic river valleys. Why? Classic river valleys have sloping sides because rain and frost have worn them away. Canyons have steep sides because they form in dry, or arid, places where

Canyon de Chelly,
Arizona

there is little rainfall to wear
down the sides.

Canyons are a lot like gorges,
but there are some differences.
Gorges have straight up-and-
down, or vertical, sides, while

the sides of canyons are usually stepped. This is because the little rain that falls in a canyon comes suddenly and all at once. So canyon rivers—and their power to erode—tend to rise and fall

Devil Canyon, Montana

Bryce Canyon, Utah

with these sudden storms. Also,
as a river cuts through a canyon,
it runs into different layers of
rock. Some of these layers are
softer than others, and are more
easily eroded away.

The Grand Canyon

The Grand Canyon is one of North America's most notable features. Cut by the Colorado River, it is 5 to 6 million years old and, at its deepest point, about 6,000 ft (1,829 m) deep.

Submarine Valleys

Valleys that lie under the surface of the ocean are said to be submarine valleys. These seafloor valleys have some of the most rugged features found anywhere on Earth.

Many submarine valleys probably were formed when the seas held less water. Glaciers and rivers

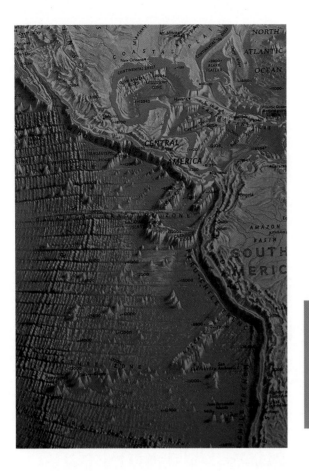

A map showing submarine valleys along North America and South America

may have eroded these valleys during ice ages of long ago. When the ice melted and the seas rose, the valleys were covered by water and became submarine valleys.

We also know that faulting action has created deep canyons where Earth's plates are being pulled apart under the sea. One such rift—the largest anywhere on Earth—is bigger than the Great Rift Valley, and it is getting bigger all the time. The Great Global Rift runs along the 40,000-mile- (64,000-km-) long mid-ocean mountain system under the major oceans of the world. But scientists cannot yet explain how all submarine valleys and canyons formed.

Canyonlands and the Green River in Utah

Whether on land or under the sea, valleys are never finished. Water and ice—and even wind—wear them down continually. The constant movement of Earth's plates is hard at work too. These forces are a reminder that our Earth is always changing.

To Find Out More

Here are some additional resources to help you learn more about valleys and canyons:

 **Books**

Parker, Steve, and Parker, Jane. **Mountains and Valleys.** Silver Dolphin, 1996.

Pope, Joyce. **The Children's Atlas of Natural Wonders.** Millbrook Press, 1995.

Rothaus, Don P. **Canyons** (Biomes of Nature Series). Child's World, 1996.

Sattler, Helen Roney. **Our Patchwork Planet: The Story of Plate Tectonics.** Lothrop, Lee & Shepard, 1995.

Sauvain, Philip Arthur. **Rivers and Valleys** (Geography Detective). Carolrhoda Books, 1996.

Organizations and Online Sites

Canadian Rockies Panoramas
http://GeoImages.Berkeley. EDU/GeoImages/QTVR/ CanadianRockies/Canadian Rockies.html

Amazing virtual-reality images of this beautiful mountain range and its valleys.

National Geographic Society at the Grand Canyon
http://www. nationalgeographic.com/ media/books/grandcanyon/ index.html

Images, an interactive map, and facts and features of the Grand Canyon.

Plate Tectonics
http://www.cotf.edu/ete/ modules/msese/ earthsysflr/plates1.html

A site explaining how movements of the Earth's plates affect land and sea.

Important Words

channel long groove or furrow

climate average weather conditions of a place over a period of years

continent one of Earth's major land areas

decaying rotting, breaking apart

eroded wore away

gouges scoops out

highlands high or hilly country

ice age period in Earth's history when large areas of land were covered by ice sheets

parallel lying in the same direction but always the same distance apart

polar having to do with the North or South Pole

sluggishly slowly

Index

Meet the Author

Larry Dane Brimner is the author of more than sixty books for children. For Children's Press, he has written books on many different topics, including *The World Wide Web, Cockroaches,* and *Caves.* Larry grew up in a valley, but now divides his time between a house on a mountain (Rico, Colorado) and one on a mesa (San Diego, California).

Harcourt Children's Books
Houghton Mifflin Harcourt
Boston New York

THE LITTLE RED PEN

Written by Janet Stevens and Susan Stevens Crummel

Illustrated by Janet Stevens

"Let's get to work!"

The Little Red Pen whirled about—
checking, circling, and marking out.

Scritch

Scratch

Scritch

"There's too much to do!
Where are my helpers?
Stapler, **Scissors**, Pencil,
Eraser, Pushpin, Highlighter!
Are you hiding in the drawer?
Get up here *now!*
If the papers aren't graded,
the students won't learn.
The school might close.
The walls might tumble.
The floors might crumble.
The sky might fall.
It might be
the end of the
world!

My back is killing me! Everybody keeps pounding on it. I could break!
I write all day, and what do I get? Sharpened down to a nub. Who needs a nub?
Don't call me Pushpin. My name is Señorita Chincheta. And I am *la última chincheta*. If I get lost—no more *chinchetas*. *¿Comprende?*

I've been cutting up all day. I'm getting dull. Not good for a sharp guy like me!
What was the question? I forget everything. My head is shrinking.
I'm bright, not crazy! Remember Mr. Felt-Tip Marker? His cap was left off, and you know where he ended up.

"The Pit of No Return!"
everyone cried.

"THE TRASH."

"Rubbish!" The Little Red Pen frowned. "You can't spend your life hiding, worrying about the Pit. There's work to be done, and I need help!"

"Well, Big Bossy Ballpoint," said Scissors, "why don't you ask Tank? He'd be a huge help."

"Tank? That lazy hamster? Never!" said the Little Red Pen. "The papers must be graded. I'll have to do it myself!"

And so she did.
Well, she tried.

Scritch

Scratch

Scritch

The Little Red Pen worked
long into the night. In the wee hours
of the morning she could barely
move across the page.

She wibbled. She wobbled.

Scritch

Scratch   Scritch

Then she fell over, exhausted. The Little Red Pen began to

r-r-r-r-r-r-o-l-l-l-l-l-l-l-l . . . . . right to the edge of the desk.

"What was that?" yelled Stapler.

"The sky is falling!" cried Pencil. "It's the end of the world!"

"No, it's not," said Highlighter. "It's probably Tank moving around in his cage."

Scissors rolled his eyes. "No way! Big Boy never moves."

"It *is* the end!" said Pencil. "I heard Pen say it. What are we going to do?"

"We're going up," snipped Scissors. "Get the lead out, Stubby!"

"Yeah," said Eraser. "Let's go . . . go . . . Where are we going? I forgot."

"To the desktop!" Chincheta shouted. *¡Vámonos! ¡Arriba, arriba!*

"¡Ay, caramba! Muchos papers!"

"Pen's *gone!*" cried Pencil. "And the papers aren't finished! The students won't learn! It's the end of the world!"

"It is *not* the end of the world," muttered Stapler.

"How do we know for sure?" asked Highlighter. "The papers have always been graded. Who knows what will happen if they're not?"

"I know!" said Eraser.

"WHAT?" They all glared.

"I forgot."

Scissors shook his head. "The end of the world could be worse than the Pit. The papers must be graded. We'll have to do it ourselves!"

And so they did.

Well, they tried.

Scissors grabbed a paper.

"No capital letter!" Clip.

"Dot that *i*!" Snip.

"Not like that!" Stapler groaned. "You cut it to shreds. Let me do it! Eraser, hop on. I see a misspelled word!" Bam! "This sentence needs a verb!" Bam! "This whole paragraph is wrong!" Bam bam bam bam bam bam!

"Not like THAT," said Highlighter. "Too many staples! Let me do it!"

Squeak squeak sque-e-e

"Not like that!" Eraser squinted. "Too bright! Let me do it!"

Rubbity rub
Smudgity smudge

"Not like that, numbskull," said Scissors. "You erased everything! Even the student's name! Whose paper is this?"

"I forgot," moaned Eraser.

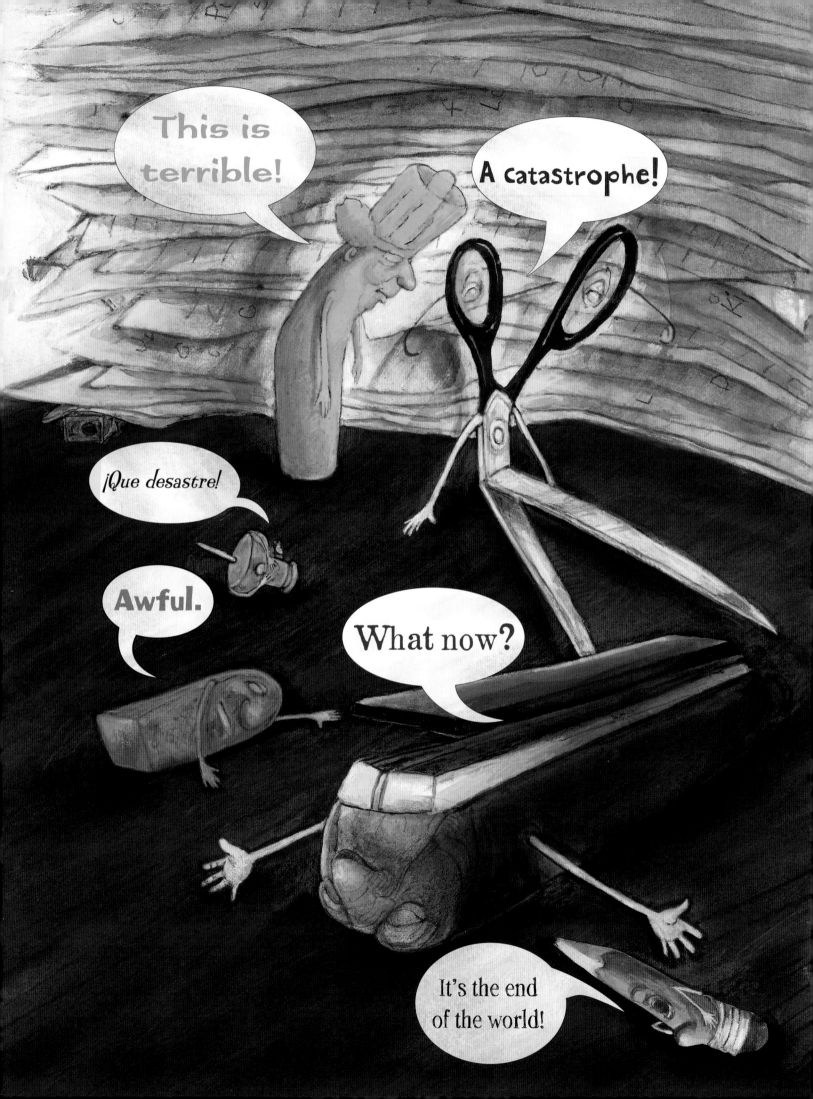

They rushed to the edge of the desk.

"Oh, no," whispered Eraser. "Pen is in the . . . the . . ."

"¡El pozo de no returno!" shouted Chincheta.

Pencil broke down. "What are we going to do? We need her. If the papers aren't graded, the students won't learn. Then they—"

"Oh, stop it already," Stapler grumbled.

"I hate to be blunt," said Scissors, "but she's a goner. No one comes back from the Pit."

"Not so fast. I have a bright idea," said Highlighter. "Paper Clip Box! Where are you? Give me your clips."

"Can't have 'em." Box scowled. "Without my clips, I'm empty. Useless. I'll end up in the—"

"OUT WITH THE CLIPS!" yelled Highlighter. "We need a chain!"

One by one,   the paper clips marched out   and hooked together.

"I know what to do!" Eraser grabbed the chain and raced across the desktop. Then he forgot to stop, bounced off the edge, and . . .

Clunk!

Hey, everybody! Guess who's down here in the Pit? The Little Red . . . uh . . . what's-her-face!

We know, rubbernoggin. Now you're both in the Pit.

"I have another bright idea," said Highlighter. "Eraser, grab the Little Red Pen. We'll pull you both up. Ready, everybody?"

"Too heavy." Scissors panted. "Any more bright ideas?"

"Yes!" cried Highlighter. "The hamster wheel! We'll hook the chain to the wheel! Then Tank will run, the wheel will turn, the chain will—"

"Whoa," Scissors cut in. "Tanky Boy hasn't been on the wheel in years. Besides, how are we going to get from here to there?"

"Ruler can be our bridge!" declared Highlighter.

"What? Me, a bridge?" Ruler snapped. "I'm not budging an inch."

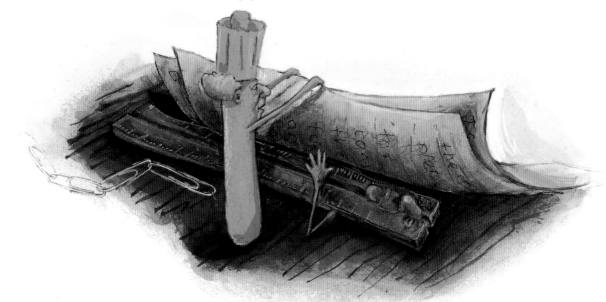

"Move it!" yelled Highlighter.

"Oh, all right." Ruler stretched out. Farther . . . farther . . . one more inch . . . half an inch . . .

Clunk!

Oh, great. Three in the Pit.

Need some help?
Yardstick! I thought you were broken and down in the—

"The Pit?" said Yardstick. "Nobody throws me in the Pit. I may be shorter now, but I'm tall enough to hold up this plant and long enough to be your bridge."

Yardstick stretched out. Farther . . . farther . . . one more inch . . . half an inch . . . He made it!

Everyone dashed across, but Pencil froze.
"I—I—I'm afraid."

"Aw, come on, Pencil! You can do it!"
said Stapler. "Don't look down!"

Sharpener peeked out from under a pile of
papers. "I'll help you."

"Ahhhhhh!" Pencil took one look at
Sharpener and bolted across.

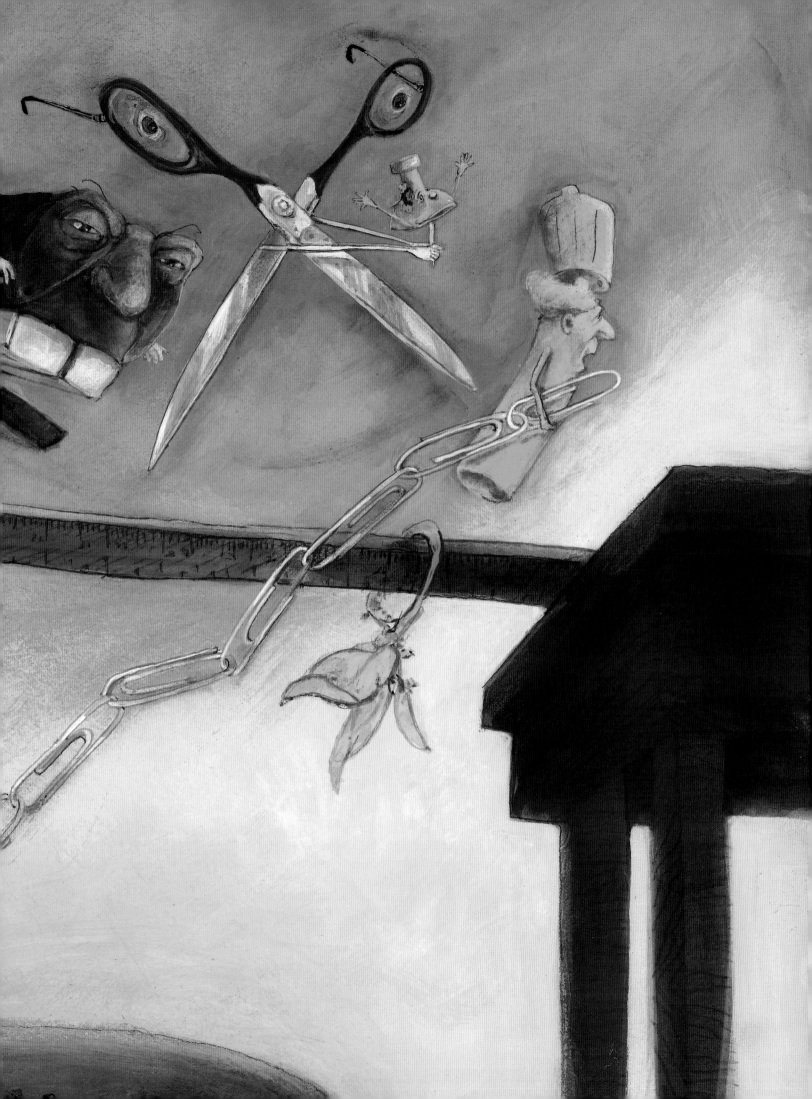

snort

snort

z-z-z-z-z-z-z-z-z-z-z-z-z-z-z-z-z-z-z-z-z-z-z-z-z-z-z-z-z-z

They opened the cage door and crept inside. Highlighter hooked the paper clip chain to the wheel. "Okay. Grab Tank. We're hauling him over."

"Hamster *grande*," Chincheta groaned. "*¡MUY grande!*"

They huffed and they puffed until finally they pulled Tank onto the wheel.
Highlighter took a deep breath. **"Wake up, Tank! Run!"**

Chincheta smiled.
"I can wake him up."

POKE!

ROARRRRRRRR!

"Tankzilla!" Pencil shrieked.
"It's the end of the world!"

Around and around.

Faster and faster.

The wheel turned.

The chain moved.

Up. Up. Up.

Up came **Ruler.**

Up came **Eraser.**

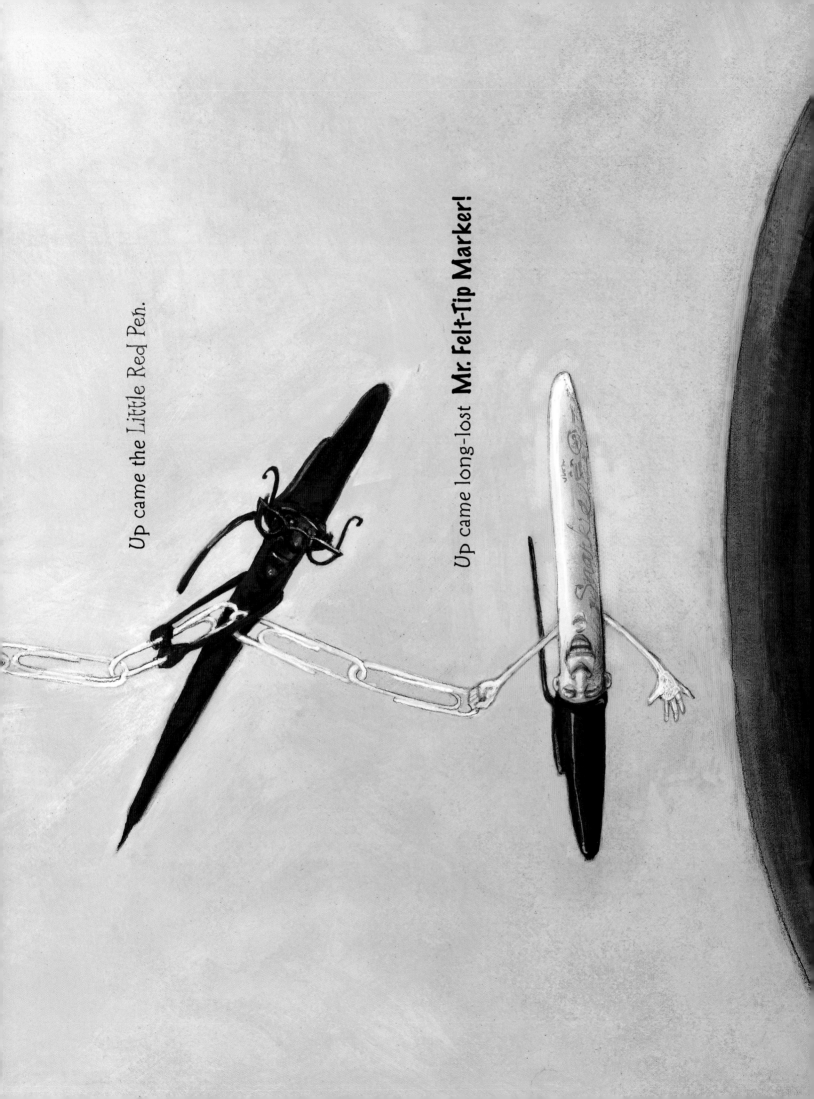

Up came the Little Red Pen.

Up came long-lost **Mr. Felt-Tip Marker!**

"It worked!" shouted Highlighter. "And we did it all by ourselves!"

Chincheta clapped. *¡Bravo!*

"Did we save the world?" asked Pencil.

The Little Red Pen beamed. "You saved *us*, but now—"

"**Now,**" said Eraser, "we have a job to finish!"

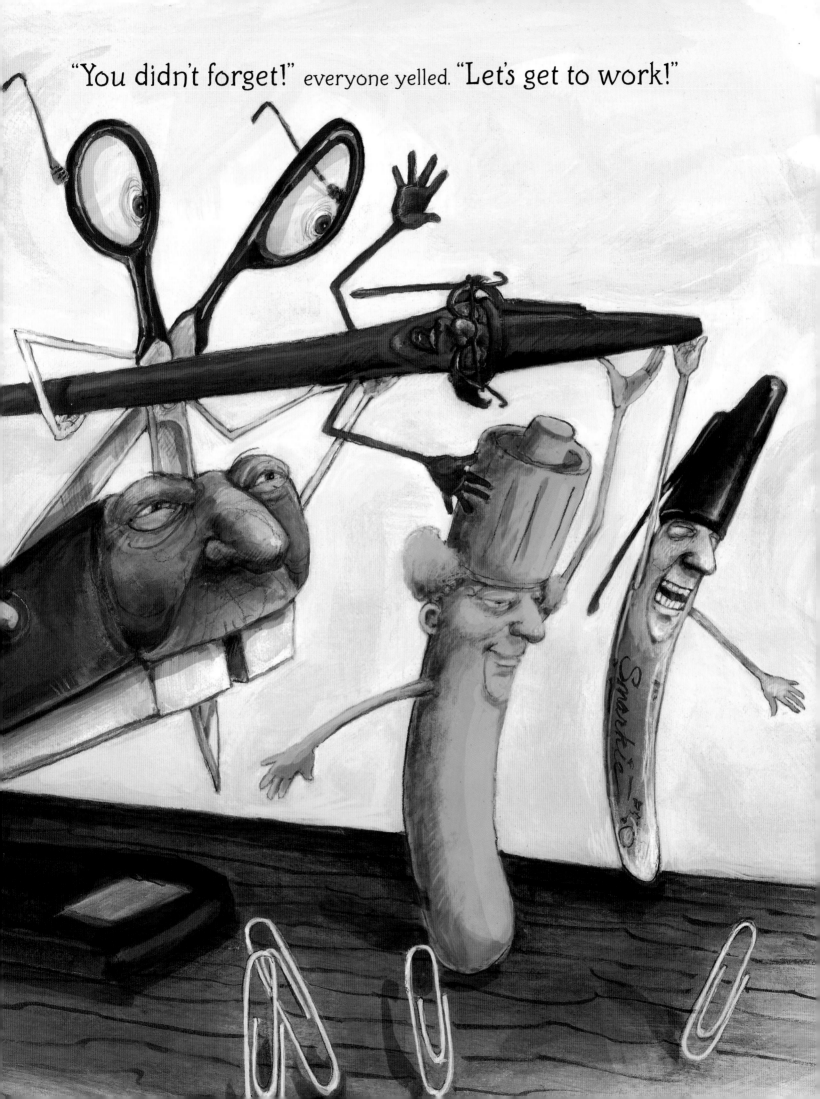

"You didn't forget!" everyone yelled. "Let's get to work!"

And so they did. They checked and stapled, organized and alphabetized, piled and filed, without another thought of running low, becoming dull, drying up, getting lost, breaking down, or landing in the Pit until the job was done.

The world was safe.

And no one hid in the drawer ever again.

Except you-know-who.

To Jeannnette, the real little Pen Red

and a great editor

—Janet and Susan

Harcourt Children's Books is an imprint of Houghton Mifflin Harcourt Publishing Company.

www.hmhco.com

The illustrations in this book were done in mixed media.
Designed by Regina Roff

Library of Congress Cataloging-in-Publication Data
Stevens, Janet.
The little red pen / written by Janet Stevens and Susan Stevens Crummel ;
illustrated by Janet Stevens.
p. cm.
Summary: When a little red pen accidentally falls into the waste basket
while trying to correct papers all by herself, the other classroom supplies must
cooperate to rescue her.
ISBN 978-0-15-206432-7
[1. Office equipment and supplies—Fiction. 2. Schools—Fiction.
3. Humorous stories.] I. Crummel, Susan Stevens. II. Title.
PZ7.S84453Li 2011
[E]—dc22
2010009062

Manufactured in China
SCP 16 15 14 13 12 11
4500796209